DREAMS AND BLESSINGS

Six Visionary Poets:

Lisha Adela Garcia
Jennifer Read Hawthorne
Anna Kodama
Nancy Lee Melmon
Angie Minkin
Suzanne Dudley

Edited by Diane Frank

Foreword by Jennifer Read Hawthorne
#1 *New York Times* bestselling coauthor
Chicken Soup for the Woman's Soul

BLUE LIGHT PRESS ◆ 1ST WORLD PUBLISHING

SAN FRANCISCO ◆ FAIRFIELD ◆ DELHI

Dreams and Blessings

Edited by Diane Frank

Blue Light Press
www.bluelightpress.com
bluelightpress@aol.com

1st World Publishing
PO Box 2211
Fairfield, IA 52556
www.1stworldpublishing.com

Book & Cover Design: Melanie Gendron

Cover Art & Illustrations: Anna Kodama

First Edition

Library of Congress Control Number: 2020936471

ISBN: 9781421836560

Dreams and Blessings

Contents

This Stone Will Speak
Poems by Lisha Adela Garcia

Wild Child
Poems by Jennifer Read Hawthorne

Barefoot in the Dust of a Dream
Poems by Anna Kodama

The Salt Water Kiss
Poems by Nancy Lee Melmon

Ancient Rains
Poems by Angie Minkin

Snapshots from the Album
of the Half-Empty, Half-Full Glass
Poems by Suzanne Dudley

Glossary

Foreword

We call ourselves Poet Sisters, connected in a web of words and visions. We dream together. Write together. Celebrate together. We share feedback, encouragement, praise, suggestions, inspiration — and so much love.

The six of us — Lisha Adela Garcia, Anna Kodama, Angie Minkin, Nancy Lee Melmon, Suzanne Dudley, and I — are all students of Diane Frank, San Francisco poet, teacher, and founder of Blue Light Press, a highly respected publisher of poetry. We come and go in Blue Light Press's three annual online workshops and an in-person summer workshop. We are a combination of serious, funny, quirky, and elegant.

Whenever any one of these women pops into my inbox, my heart skips in delightful anticipation of the poem I'm about to read. It might be poignant or humorous or deep or mystical — but always authentic. And it will open my eyes to a new and unexpected way of perceiving the world.

When they tell me how much they love a line I've written, I trust them. When they say they're not sure about something I've written, I trust that, too. When I have doubts about my writing, they set me straight and say the perfect thing to get me going again. And they give me permission to do the same for them.

Our poems take us deeper, show us what we value, help us explore the themes of our lives. We write to understand ourselves better — and to explain the world we live in. We write to understand how all beings connect, in this world and beyond. To capture the ineffable beauty of a leaf, a sacred body of water, the colors of birds, the sounds of trees, our deepest feelings. We write to celebrate what is good in the world and why we would like our planet to survive.

Sometimes it feels like an impossible struggle, a kind of private and very small but necessary treasure hunt, in which we don't even know what we're searching for — until we find it.

We write of children, animals, dreams, triumphs, and loss. We write about social injustice, our histories, our conflicts, our pain. We write about everyday life — as one poet put it, attempting to capture the universe in a tabby cat trying to catch a monarch butterfly in the morning sun. She'll never catch it, but she never stops leaping. And neither will we.

Poetry is the language of the soul. We are honored that you are drawn to this work, which we offer in heartfelt gratitude, knowing that our circle expands through you and all who appreciate language and the gift of poetry to express the essence of life.

Jennifer Read Hawthorne

This Stone Will Speak

Poems by Lisha Adela Garcia

My Mother Wants Me to Explain

For Dr. Adela Artola Allen

My mother wants me to write poems
about the different borders between
Anglo and Mexican culture.
No amamos igual, no sentimos igual.

Tell how most Americans
don't laugh at death or write *Calaveras*
about the President, or make tamales at Christmas.

Explain when non-Mexicans buy
every ingredient fresh to cook our food,
the chile against their skin,
their tongue, can never taste the conquest,
write about that.

My poems are about what unites us, I reply,
heart to eyes, throat to guttural survival.

But we still speak the language of Cervantes
she counters, Cervantes and Nahuatl, Zapotec
Purepecha and Mayan. They speak
in Northern, Southern or Midwestern.

Explain the importance of the hands
of women who choose to tell their stories
in the colors of their *huipiles*
and wouldn't dream of looking the same
store after store, mall after mall.

Speak with your fingers to tell the story
of coyotes and owls,

why birds always arrive in the Americas,
and carry spirits on their wings.

Tell why hatred
for differences has also claimed us,
why it is important
that bougainvilleas have thorns.

Speak for all of us still here,
and for those who have been here
so long they have lost their Spanish,
who hear the Mariachis, the cantos,
and have forgotten the nuances of our songs.

A Woman's Hands in a Time of War

"Let the rubble be our evidence..." — Heather McHugh

When I place my hands together,
meeting palm against palm, and press
so hard my knuckles turn white,
I know I have squeezed the screams

out of my prayers. Together, all the women
I know force their hands onto
their abdomens, a mother's signal
to God that our wombs

crave new seedlings, bread.
War is too long,
dreaming, the only reality.
A man from America took a picture

of me once, placing both my hands
on the space between my birth
button and my husband's peace,
pressing so hard that hope escaped along

with the hunger. My hands change
positions often, clutching stones to throw
at the stray men who prey on our children
or to scare the vultures nearby. These hands

molded clay into water jars before
and now, they carry bodies with faces
I do not know, wrapped in scraps for the heaps
to be sorted later. I hope other women will

do this for my love, for my village.
My fingers curve to write the words that hold
my skin onto a sheet of paper, a letter that gets folded
over and over as if holding my love, has limits

within the creases. When I get angry at God,
my hands tighten into fists and I hit my thighs
and do not breathe.
I fear the life I hold in might escape

with the tears. I strap my breasts down
with cloths left over from birthing
dead babies. I visit the old graves of the city
and make room for the new.

My grandmother lived through war, and she said
sometimes it takes years before the layers in the rubble
reveal the underbelly of why
it was worth living at all.

"A Woman's Hands in a Time of War" received the Brodine-Brodinsky Poetry Prize in 2008.

This Stone Will Speak

As the high Maya priestess of Chichén Itzá,
I rule the temple, and I am dying.
Before I leave, I have carved a stela
of all my mistakes, to be placed
on the east wall of the nunnery.
It is hell revealed, my life.

This is the only way to escape the priests,
my tribe and the indifference of heaven
that has tethered minds
to the tradition of human sacrifice.

My story is bordered in the skulls
of the warriors that gave their
lives for the poets.
When my bones have burned
and I enter the chrysalis of heaven,
my errors will be placed in plain view.

What I have hidden
will be revealed
in stone that faces the sunrise.

What I have endured
will be remembered
in stone that shadows with sunset.

All will know why at the end,
I stood alone with the *quetzal*
to be burned.

Immigration Social Worker

She is the kind of bird
indifferent to plumage —
earth tones: brown, black and the palest blue.

Hair cut practical.
No time for fashion or a man's caress
when humanity is peeling its own flesh.

Her eyes translate into language,
the detritus of feet
that walked three thousand miles to safety.

We are all children of Eve
biting different parts of apple —
knowledge to suit our beliefs.

But God made the apple whole
and poisoned the politics of service
in the name of Yahweh.

She gathers papers and wraps identity
on wristbands in case they get separated.
Her charges are the music

of blue monarchs finding sanctuary,
and she is the tired
white dove's instrument.

The Day We Split in Two — Entering the USA

You'll learn English and the proper way to say, "Yes, Sir!"

At midnight, fleeing my father
in the back seat of a Rambler
station wagon, life escapes
into my mother's bruises
as a sullen driver speeds us north.

Trumpet notes bloom
from the radio,
lodge into her clavicle,
breath upon breath.

At high speed, around
mountain curves
and miles of gravel,
we hope to cross
the Sierra Madre before dawn.

Rancor for dreams left in the rains of Mexico City
settles into her eyes.

How will I survive this lower altitude
split in two,
our spirits vaporizing
into the rocks of the *cordillera*?

The cigarette smoke paths
she still craves in sleep
bind her fear — tattoo her face.

From this day forward,
her words,
full of hidden ordnance.

Texas Courtship in the Rio Grande Valley

I search for the thermos of pink
lemonade. The moccasin
swims the surface of the pond at my back.
Black satin poison and slither surprise
for the white man courting my mother
with a picnic on his ranch.

She tells me about the dignity of chaparral
and mesquite as the land yields
to a marsh with gray-brown and yellow birds,
anis, pygmy owls and kiskadees.
All this land for just a few cows
who still cross the border in the Rio
Grande Valley undisturbed.

He talks about the grasshopper infestation.

I tell myself she is an artist,
a ballet dancer
from Mexico City. She will never
bring me to live here.

His pearly buttons shine with the light
from the muddy water. He bends
casually for the morning paper,
only it's a rifle. He shoots the snake
in the head — its opalescent white mouth
flowers open for an instant,
now a carcass of red and black
left for the vultures.

Welcome to Texas, he smiles,
home of the swimmer snakes.

Ven hija.

A New Pond

I want to be the gentle gnaw on apple skin
a brown mark on yellow flesh — still delicious.
More than just bread crumbs on pink lips
or a passing light on stones
that warms hardness.

A Kokopelli flute
to play silhouette against
an orange harvest moon.

I want purple and teal to be primary colors,
explain why I am a Degas
among Warhols. A *gitana*
who turns each day's iron nails
into appreciation for the discordant.

I can be a love nude
unblemished, without scissor scars,
with a word trail in my wake
that outlasts gray's mediocrity.

The sound in an untenable tuning fork,
the creator of green verbs
that vibrate beyond dreams.

I will be a lavender jacaranda blossom
who kisses the sun
and then falls asleep by yellow
patches of moon on Saltillo tile.

Gather

Gather my hands now that they are spotted.
Move slowly over the knots growing on the knuckles.
Grasp my fingers together as if they were scented tulips
emerging red from winter's hibernation

       bent in a loose curve,
       stroking your forehead to sleep,
       or to close the eyes of your beloved grandmother
       from this world to spirit.

              Take my hands to the bark of a birch,
              to hear once again the lullaby of ants
              and green wood bending to a gust.
              Give me a virgin page and a purple pen
      so that I may rediscover the white ledge of possibility.

Hold my scars so you don't repeat them.
Gather apple blossoms and place them
on my chest, beneath prayerful hands.
I won't forget, but one day,
you might long for their weight.

La Llorona

Take me to the river of your weeping *Llorona*.
Spare a star from the silence
embroidered on your white *huipil*.
I am El Negro, the black one who loves you.

A star from your silence drifts
in moonlight between cemetery stones.
I am the black one who sees you, *Llorona*,
the one death hasn't touched.

Owls call the moonlight on cemetery stones
and lie about the dead not making noise.
I am the one death has forgiven its touch
in the river of your eternal mourning.

The dead moon lies about the keening noise,
the whispered enchantments of your pale lips.
Take me to the cold river of mourning
as currents purge the bones of our children.

Whisper enchantments from your pale lips
to warn mothers of your nightly visits.
Currents purge the bones of our children
each time I cross a son on the Rio Grande,

Warn the mothers of the coyote visits
when leaving the sheets of their birth.
Each time I lose a son on the Rio Grande,
tell them El Negro hears owls call their name.

Three Months in the USA

On Bear Mountain, the Mayan refugees of Los Angeles gather to pray for my children. I have been released to my uncle Jorge, who fled the slaughters of the Guatemalan Army in our village 35 years ago. They killed most of our family with their new U.S. Army machine guns. Doña Jacinta clears the last of our auras with blue vine sage before beginning the drumming circle. Around us copal burns in incense clay containers that cannot spark the forest, to seal us in protection.

We are among redwoods, incense cedar and ponderosa pines, seated on blankets, clearing our minds for the summoning. A red-tailed hawk perches above me on a branch. My hand is dyed in the form of a spiked magenta star that will eventually fade. A talisman for finding a child like the one that shone over Bethlehem centuries ago. The rattles and drums begin their collective heartbeats to beckon the ancestors, saints and spirits for clarity and favors.

I last held my children at the border, where I turned myself in to the men in green and told them I was seeking refuge, fleeing the drug violence and the death of my husband. They took my Ernesto age 5 and Trini age 3 to take a video. They never brought them back. My husband died refusing to fight for the cartels. He bade us leave before our children too were killed as an example to others who refuse to join the gangs. I came here to save our lives, my feet still bleeding from the three-month walk.

I do not hear the call to the ancestors and angels of good. I hear the drug lord's chants in the drumbeats. *The gringos need drugs, the gringos need drugs.* This is life in the highlands of Guatemala; there is nothing else. We thought when we reached the Rio Bravo, Rio Grande, the large river of courage, we could breathe safety. We were thirsty, hungry and fleeing the coyotes who kept hounding our heels.

They sent me on a bus to a shelter with cages. Won't tell me where my children are. I have lost my words. I have Ernesto's asthma medicine in my bag and purple ribbons for Trini's braids. Three weeks later they released me to Uncle Jorge. He has brought me here with the elders. The drums continue their prayer in search of a miracle to find my children. They are in another state in this country of gigantic greed. *Stay strong*, the elders say. I just want the razor.

Pour *Quetzalteca* on the ground.
Pour tobacco on the ground
for the sacred mother of us all.

The hawk's cries lift from my chest.
I watch as it breaks a dove's neck.

In the Coconino Forest around Sedona

Sudden silence
　　in the usual hum of the forest.

A predator, perhaps an owl.
　　No one wants to call attention or be a target,

but it speaks to your ear alone.

You know it is not an enchantment,
　　but a message beyond
　　　　the breath of a body.

It is the effort of an angel
embracing a moment
　　to tap you on the shoulder,
　　　　bring transparent feathers to cup your cheeks
　　　　　　and ask you to remember being loved.

No belonging to solitude
　　but to a grander forest
　　　　of endless ancestors
　　　　　　walking a desert to surround you.

Hard labor
　　is required
　　　　daily in an unloving world.

　　Your body needs the scent of the Blue Spruce,
　　　　Ponderosa and Piñon.

　　The world's choirs require your participation.

Every white calla lily
      has pollen from its yellow pistil
          on its body.

We wear and shed the jackets of years
      and now towards the end,
          fear the loneliness
              of pine needles discarded on the path.

Do not be comfortable
      alone with the gray,
          wrinkles around your eyes,
              the loss of quick movements and speed.

Feel your grandmother long gone from this soil
      hold one of your hands
          above the clouds
              as your feet continue on the ground.

Use your remaining mornings
      to assist
          younger travelers
              over familiar boulders.

Be the rushing water of Oak Creek
      when cardinals finally settle on your shoulders.

Maria Elena at the Salvation Army

Hola Magdalena,

I haven't seen you since your *quinceañera*. I heard you went to college in San Antonio. I am surprised you recognized me, as the furrows of the fields now dance on my face. I like to think of my wrinkles as ripening under the sun, like the strawberries and jalapeños I used to pick. The family moved to El Cenizo by the river. It is smaller than Laredo and peaceful except when the drug gangs shoot their machine guns at night. Do you remember my grandson Pablo? He brings me once a month to the Salvation Army for a food box. I now get the vegetables and fruit I used to pick fresh, in cans. We don't follow the crops anymore.

Yes, you can take my picture. So, you work for a newspaper and readers are interested in *viejitas* like me? I don't mind standing against the stucco wall. Look at my hand. I am proud that my fingers have not curled into talons with arthritis. So many of us can't easily move after 40 years in the fields. My eyes took in the clouds with cataracts, but I can still see the faces of my grandchildren, and that is all that matters.

Remember when you used to run to my house so I could braid your hair before Mass while your mother dressed the twins? My *trenzas* are thin but they still tap my shoulders when I walk. Your mother comes to see me once in a while and brings me beautiful *batas* to wear that she sews herself. I have gotten so boney that I can only wear these housecoats, as everything else falls off.

Ándale Magdalena, que Dios te bendiga. Give my *saludos* to your mother. Send me a copy of the picture so my family can remember me.

Niño Perdido
Mariachi Moment

*Anonymous composer from Sonora, Mexico around
1920. Most likely La Concordia Band*

A trumpet duet and song ask
where are you my son?
I have asked the wind to slant the rain in your direction.

Trumpet notes seek you
down the cobblestones
behind the church
around the Alameda
on the road to Hermosillo.

I am not a pretty hummingbird that gives up its heart.
I am an eagle that flies as high as the clouds over the Sierra Madre,

over the ocean,
all the way to the holy land.
Don't be deceived by the Mockingbird
who steals my voice
to lure you further away.

I hear your own trumpet calling me.
Your blood will sing when I am near,

your skin will prick against your white shirt.
I know it is terrifying
that the walls of our home in Los Alamos
can hold my spirit for 300 years.
Search for me. I will hear you.

Ask the Archangel Gabriel to play his horn.
Your mother is not a dream.

Blue Sheets

So many years tucking kids in blue sheets,
preparing *frijoles* and *sopa de fideo*.
Strong while paying bills
on a single mom's food budget,
and all I really wanted

was to baptize my eyes with Rumi
and age without a sound.
I wanted more as a mother
than to be an old woman
wearing her rosaries.

I face head on the addiction
of numbness
when I bury the elders
while schooling the young.
When *la droga* of too much
makes me suspicious of God
and threatens to erase
my contour from the landscape,
I rebel.

I write and write
and read and write till flesh
on my bones fills with color
and my lungs breathe
in rhythm with the stars.

Once death's cloak discarded my family
from the night itself,
from the stems of nightmares.
Once the kids left home

and left empty their closets,
I knitted the abandonment in letters
and adopted just one more dog.

I am back to tucking in blue sheets
during lightning storms
as the dogs seek shelter
around the books and notebooks
that surround me as I sleep.

My Grandmother's Sugar Bowl

Buddha belly round and delighted
in the gold foliage painted on its surface
in the 1850's. Lattice around delicate
roses without thorns

are a window into the white sweetness of cane.
Dignified to rest on the brown and black
granite kitchen counter, owning its space
as if planted in soil.

A visit to the night kitchen
a careless gesture searching for the tea tin
behind it and all that history shatters.

A failed government in the proud
government of sugar
scatters its refugees —
never the same,
so hard to lift up.

In the Market, In the City

after William Carlos Williams

In a hurry to reach the meat stall
where everything must be fresh,
the butcher's assistant dodges
pot holes and people.

Brown hands with dirty fingernails grasp
the handles of the red wheelbarrow
filled with hog's heads.

A knife with a brown handle
is lodged between one
set of eyes, blood still
on the knife. Nothing wasted.

White chickens hang upside down
by their feet. Shoppers squeeze
thighs through feathers
and feel the juice and flavor of a meal.

Chicken feet are served
in the next stall, fried
over a coal stove mixed with spices
and sauces ready wax paper.

Monsoon rains come early,
glaze the windows of cars
parked in the street. A small sparrow
drinks from a puddle of mud.

Police sirens flash red and white lights,
hurry to catch a suspect
nearby. The noise
stops suddenly. A stray dog howls.

Watching everything inside this painting,
the boy sits on the curb across the street
waiting for his mother
as she bargains the price of squash.

Tar stains his new Nike tennis shoes.
So much depends on what he sees
and the red and white can of Coke
he holds in his hand.

Wild Child

Poems by Jennifer Read Hawthorne

Ripening

Fullness is on me
like the taste of watermelon in summer.
My remaining days stretch out
like a carpet of ripe pecans
on the floor of the orchard
behind my grandparents' house,
each one waiting to be
picked up, cracked open, savored.
No more youthful hunger;
I eat the moonrise over the ocean,
my mouth round with silver.

My Mother's House

I stand at the door of my mother's house,
hand on the doorbell,
longing to hear the chimes
that once set dogs barking.
But what will I say if the new owner answers the door?

I could show him the patch of front yard
near the pecan tree,
where the white clover was always thickest —
where my sisters and I raced to see
who could catch the most honeybees
in the Ball jars our mother gave us.
We added grass and clover blossoms,
punched holes in the gold metal lids
so the bees could breathe,
dozed in the sweet grass
to their musical murmuring,
while the sun turned our skin
the color of honey.

I could point out the stand of longleaf pines
in the far corner of the backyard —
or what's left after sixty years of summer storms.
He's looked at them many times, of course,
but has he ever lain on the thick carpet
of lemon-scented needles in the middle of the copse,
thick with fairies dancing on every branch?

Over there's the wisteria that spills
across the bones of beloved family animals.
And the mimosa tree — Panther Girl's refuge
in times light and dark,

widespread limbs that welcomed me
to stretch out, bask, press my face into flowers,
drunk on the sweet scent of pink feather blossoms
and Louisiana summers.

My fingers press the bell.
The door opens.
Hello, I say. *I used to live here.*

Wild Child

I gave my soul a name.
Wild Child, I call her
or sometimes Sweet Child,
in the night.
Sugar, when I'm feeling Southern.

Wild was the girl
who lay in the white clover,
drunk on summer sun
and the clean smell of grass.
She'd roll onto her belly,
press her cheek against the ground,
cradled, like an infant
in the arc of its mother's neck,
fiercely protected, wildly content.

I want to lie with Life like this,
head resting on God's breast,
our pulses throbbing in unison,
fearless.

We can do this, Sugar.

Touchstone

Winter in the Deep South never lasted
more than four days at a time.
Those days, we walked to school
in thin little dresses
covered by thin little coats —
bare legs, bare hands, bare heads —
as if the thought of pants or gloves or hats
might appear concessional,
an invitation for winter to stay.

One day, squeezing my small frame smaller
against the cold, hands numb
clutching books and Cinderella lunchbox,
I made the painful three-block journey
from bus stop to home.
This is the coldest day of my life
and I'm NEVER going to forget it.
The shivery vow burned
into my six-year-old mind.

Awareness looks back,
recognizes Itself,
unchanging thread, child to elder.
Vibrating in the hum of the Eternal,
I feel the cold and laugh.

Easter Morning on Black Mountain

We were thinking of going to church
but first had to stick our noses out Candace's front door
to see if our Florida blood could meet the demands
of cold mountain air, chilled bones.

The first rays of sunlight, but there,
on the porch, a small square package,
wrapped in plain pink paper,
two fuchsia azaleas scotch-taped to the top.

Rose, Candace said, and showed us a photo
of her young friend, the mountain girl
who lived next door, just back
from a family trip to the Carolina shore.

Inside the box, four shells —
a calico scallop, a sundial, and a marsh periwinkle,
neatly stacked and covered
by the copper-colored back of a horseshoe crab.

I pictured the clear-eyed shell seeker
reaching down to examine a moon snail
while other 12-year-olds clutched their phones,
felt a surge of hope.

Goodness, gentleness, and love
in a little pink box,
a perfect sermon for Easter morning
on Black Mountain.

The Yogini

She eases into Triangle Pose,
feet wide, hugging the tangerine mat,
arms wide awake, stretching
between heaven and earth
like a tilted Vitruvian Woman.

She checks her alignment —
imperceptible shift of hips —
presses her back body gently
against an imagined plane.

Her gaze rides an outflow of breath
upward to her reaching hand,
follows the line of light
from fingertips to the point
at the center of the celestial arc.

Heart open, she breathes in the stars.

The Wedding

What is left to say at the wedding
after fifteen years together,
what is left to marry?

Medicine woman, the thought flashed
the instant I first saw you.
So different, we two,
yet our hands closed perfectly
around each other.

Fingers entwined, we walked for years
along sandy beaches,
to set our feet in one direction.
We lay on our backs in Atlantic waters,
grasping hands in the vastness,
surrendering conflict to the currents
sweeping out to sea.

You made medicine from gemstones,
and we swallowed diamonds, white sapphires,
drinking ourselves into a state of beauty
that withstood all loss and sorrow.

Now here we stand,
in the Christ garden,
inside a sacred wood.
The ceremony begins.
A thousand bamboo stalks
quiver in ecstasy.

Surgical Vision

She filled me with her blue-diamond essence,
promised protection —
I will be at your head,
my son, the Christ, at your feet.

She introduced my celestial guardians —
Lithusia, standing on my left
in raiment of dawn blue edged in navy,
Anna Mae to my right in light-suffused rose.
Large angels, she added.

St. Germain will be your surgeon,
and at my request,
Archangel Raphael will hold us all
in the healing of sacred time and space.

She was right about all of it.
Not even the veil of anesthesia
could block the grace of these light beings
from permeating my body and soul.
They came and have not left.

Beneath the Radar

Some of my friends are famous.
They might dine with a European princess,
share the stage with Sir Richard Branson,
be granted an audience with the Dalai Lama.

I slipped into a smaller life.
A tiny sliver at the edge of the continent.
Why go to India when my eyes can travel
all the way to Earth's curve in no-time,
2.9 miles from my sea-striped beach chair
across rolling, breathing, Atlantean aquamarine.

My thoughts are like breaths now.
They rise, then fall into stillness,
like the gap at the end of an exhale.
I am in love with this quiet place.
It lets me hear the palm trees singing.
It writes my poems.

Memorial Day

The sea had laid a carpet of broken shells
across the sand, a billion memorials
to fallen creatures of the deep.
Her feet reveled in the rough texture,
while her eyes sought the softness
of conch-colored pinks, her favorites
except for the pieces of alabaster white,
smooth and stained with amethyst.

Low tide, and the snowbirds
had fled for the summer,
the beach a luxury of emptiness.
How do you stand the heat?
they always wanted to know.

She leaned down to finger a ridged fragment
of pink shell, an angel's wing
that she slipped into her pocket,
a marker, like a thousand others,
of a day she wanted to remember.

Out of Bounds

In a dream, she unzipped her skin suit,
stepped out of her soul-home,
floated, widened, rose.
A few flyovers, fast and low
like the Blue Angels,
then she settled into orbit,
studied the dwelling below.

At once, seven billion heartbeats
vibrated her body in a pulse of singularity.
She could smell the scent of newborns
washed clean by their mothers,
taste the sweetness dripping from honeysuckle vines,
hear the wings of a trillion butterflies.

The only divides she could see
between blue and red
were sapphire and cerulean river ribbons
that cut through brick-colored deserts,
the red clay of Mississippi,
the burning rocks of Zion.

In the morning, when she landed,
she opened the door onto a new world.

Authors Ridge

Authors Ridge is a section of Sleepy Hollow Cemetery in Concord, Massachusetts.

The names on the stones
at the top of the hill
are noble — Emerson,
Thoreau, Alcott, Hawthorne.
So little space their bodies take,
sons and daughters asleep
for ages with their families,
giants in simple graves,
marked by the offerings
of wayfarers — pens, pencils,
scribbled lines of favorite verses.

It's quiet in Sleepy Hollow,
but on Authors Ridge, no death.
Words flash between tombstones,
as the voices of the great writers
reach across the centuries
to tell their tales of little women,
scarlet letters, Walden Pond,
the Revolution.

I place my pen across Louisa May's name,
joy in my pilgrim's heart.

The Beauty of Him

He was left alone in his wheelchair
at the edge of the physical therapy room,
head bowed, broken.
She studied him as she willed her legs
to lift the weights around her ankles.

About seventy, she guessed,
and he looked like a Spanish nobleman.
Silver hair combed straight back
from his honey-colored face,
gray designer jeans and matching hoodie
over a spotless white shirt,
sandals with wide, crisscrossing bands
a shade lighter than his golden skin.

I want to meet him, she thought,
and slipped onto her own wheels
to roll across the floor.
Mr. Sanchez, she said. His head lifted.
She rested her hand lightly on his arm,
took in the beauty of him.
I love the way you look.

He can't see you, the therapist said,
and he speaks only Portuguese.
But the old man covered her hand
with his and smiled.

In Search of Mary Oliver

1.

A few lines of Mary Oliver,
and she begins to cry.
Her own morning light
doesn't fall on coreopsis —
it highlights the neighbor's car
encroaching on her parking space.
She can't hear birds' wings overhead —
high-impact windows protect
against hurricanes and Florida heat
and every sweet sound of birds and tree frogs.

2.

When she was a child, a hurricane meant
a sleepover at her best friend's house.
Her parents let them stand on the veranda,
watch the winds lash the oak trees,
feel the spray of wind-whipped water,
twirl their bodies in a whirlwind of glee.
She spent half her childhood
face down in pink clover,
white pine needles, breathing dirt.

3.

November. The in-between time,
when you can throw open the house,
inhale the smell of sunlight
before the heat stifles every thought.
A few lines of Mary Oliver
and she unlatches every door and window,

listens as the house fills with music —
cardinals, jays, mourning doves.

She resolves to go to the beach,
count the brown pelicans flying south,
lie on the sand beside a sea turtle's nest,
feel the heartbeat of a hundred babies
waiting to be born.

Taking My Measurements

I wonder if on my deathbed
I'll have time to calculate
the exact midpoint of my life —
reflect on where I was at that moment
and what I was doing, oblivious
that I had just completed
the first half of my life.

If this seems weird, just know that
I get immense pleasure from measuring things,
like how long it takes to make the king-size bed —
two minutes, in case you're wondering.

Or counting the number of stairs
from my condo at the top of the building
to the ground floor – two flights of eighteen,
I should add, which always makes me feel
triumphant when I go the other way
and labor at the top for only six breaths.

This is good to know because I remember
hearing about two Indian astrologers
visiting the town where I used to live,
aghast to see a runner flying by
as they were on their evening stroll —
Doesn't he know that life is measured
in breaths?

That explains a lot, but on second thought,
I don't think I'll be measuring much
on my deathbed. If I'm lucky,
I'll be looking into the eyes of my beloved,
staring at the face of Love —
infinite, timeless, and utterly immeasurable.

What Will Happen to the Stories?

The platinum wedding ring is engraved
with my father's name, *Lowell, 14 December 1946.*
A happy day, when my parents didn't know
that a year later, he would be gone.

An antique case in my dresser drawer
holds their promise now, my own band
from a long-ago wedding tucked away
in a nearby velvet box, alongside the sixpence
that was supposed to bring good luck.

What will happen to the stories when I'm gone?
My husband gave me this scarf for my birthday.
My little boy made these turquoise and gold earrings for me.
My great-grandmother drank from this teacup.

Our children pine for nothing of the past.
They drop a thousand dollars for an Apple watch —
who needs the simple timepiece awarded
Grandfather for a lifetime of hard work?

The pair of candlesticks?
No one wants to polish silver anymore.
Or bother to remember the Russian colonel
who presented them to my parents as a wedding gift.

Someone will sort it all into piles –
secrets, dreams, family history
headed for distant nephews and nieces,
auction, recycling, The Salvation Army.

Until then, I will keep the stories,

of tiny objects hidden in the corners of a dresser,
symbols of lives and love, loss and joy,
vessels for the meaning we all yearn for.

Barefoot in the Dust of a Dream

Poems by Anna Kodama

Sophia, Awake in the Middle of the Night

Tonight the world is small.
It fits inside my womb.
I walk in shafts of moonlight
on the painted floor.
Each step rocks my pelvic cradle,
earth bones of oceanic weight.

Once, I was weightless.
I rode the blue mare belly down
through boundless waves of space.
My breastbone fused to her muscled neck.
My hair tangled in her silver mane.
Galloping was a necessary beauty,
my only task to hold on.

But light became matter.
Mother? Lord?
You who separates the rider from the ride
delivered me into the earth
and disappeared.
Out of minerals,
I grew monuments to appease you
and crystal words to draw you in.
I carried everything
to the top of the mountain,
waiting for the blue mare's return
and calling to you in every language
until my song drifted to dust.

I am pregnant
with accretions of the past.
I need your hurricanes

and lightning fires
to induce this still birth.
You need me to make you holy.

Labyrinth

They were just rocks
until crowbarred out of the earth
and brushed clean.
When I placed them
in a keyhole spiral
on a smooth sea of river gravel
poured and spread
over a broad clearing
prepared long ago
by a boy,
as a place to watch deer,
they became
Sentries. Witnesses. Stones.
Anyone can walk between
and turn into prayer.

Catch and Release

...a *Beautiful Nothing.*
Deserving a capital letter.

— Wisława Szymborska

The baby you are nursing arches his spine
and turns into a fish.
You wake up still human.
Your most tender skin
not even scratched by his rigid dorsal
or bruised by the muscular slapping tail.

Nothing remains
but sloughed off moonlit scales
in a dusty corner of blue linoleum.

Nothing in the birch wood cradle
carved from a single burr.

Long ago, you learned to stand on mother's lap,
then walk on solid ground.
Your feet cracked and brimmed
with deep time flecks
of 4-billion-year-old earth.

When saltwater poured out of your womb,
a sweet grass world was born
into air perfumed by your sweat,
milking your breasts
rejoicing flesh to flesh.

But you have swum enough New Hampshire ponds
to remember water
and the warm granite boulders where you stretched.
Now in this predawn hour,

with the hook in your tongue,
you recall the body's dark silhouette
the moment before it evaporates
in the sun.

In Your Shoes

Today, I wore your green and brown sneakers
and made your tracks in the soft mud of the Birthday Trail
through Hoffmann's woods and over Wolf Rock.

I kept Ben on the lead as we crossed the power cut
and yanked him back from a startled fawn,
all tiny speckled bones
and beating heart in the tall grass.

In Ulmer's greening fields, he ran free
and sailed like Rudy, over hummocks to the cow pond.
When the goslings' mother came on like a jet ski,
he dodged her and nailed a groundhog
in the ragged rows of corn stubble.

I heard its shrill whistle and click.
I watched Ben's tail flick up when he pounced.
He shook the creature twice,
then flung it high into a wide blue space,
where it slowly somersaulted
and arched its back, silently stroking upward
as if air were water and groundhogs swim.

Maybe they do.
Ben leapt and caught it in his eager jaws.
He bowed and braced his hind legs
and thrashing joyously back and forth,
made his whole body wag
with brute and beautiful delight.
I stood mute as your old shoes,
in miles and miles of missing you.

How Many Eels Does It Take to Make
a Lasting Landscape?

I didn't know eels live in Durham Creek
until a posse of naturalists waded upstream,
zapping the water with battery-powered wands
that beeped like cicadas.

Fish float belly up.
Sleek yellow elvers uncurled from the silt
and lay like pencils to be measured on a plate.
Length and numbers proved the water pure enough
to certify a Lasting Landscape.

I used to walk the banks of that crooked stream
while a five-year-old kid
with boots and a plastic bucket
dragged a stick through the water,
flipping over rocks, reaching under rotting logs,
trapping whatever wriggled through his fingers,
and pouring them all back
before the long walk home.

Home is a thing you teach your kids:
the fox in his den, bird in her nest,
boy in a gray clapboard house
with his mother and father.

If you didn't teach home,
would they ever know?
First drawings are portraits of the self.
A child's eyes look out a circle face.
The tiny crooked rectangle of home
crawls later from the crayon box,
teetering on a wobbly line
at the very bottom of the page.

Now they have found these eels,
but the naturalists worry they will not stay.
We need to keep them
fifteen or twenty years, of an age
to swim down the Delaware River,
across the Atlantic Ocean,
3000 miles to breed and die
in the green Sargasso Sea
where they were born.

When someone leaves
their muddy boots to dry
and makes an impossible journey
from which they never return,
is the Lasting Landscape
still home for the rest of us?

Oriole Nest

A math problem falls out of my bird book.
Faint writing on a square paper
in a hand I don't recognize:
Find the volume of the solid.
Lines that follow are as mysterious to me
as the tablature of bird calls.
But the long *S* hook
repeating itself down the page
exactly mimics the broken branch I'm holding.
And the smooth cup of parentheses
gathering in the scratchy little numbers
to be squared, plus and minus,
could be the soft gravid sac,
empty and dangling by its neck.

Only the oriole knows her order of operations.
How many eggs she laid
and whether they hatched and flew
before the tree let go.
But the bird's high clear voice sings
in the warp and weave of milkweed tendril,
blond hair and indestructible threads
pulled from an old blue tarp.

Here are the sides you can lean against.
Here is the hollow place
where we will gather,
you and I.
Perhaps
briefly.
Far out on the branch
of this scarlet oak,
we may hang a moment
between earth and heaven.

Prayer of the People

When the thing is born
born of yourself, born
— Charles Olson

Where do we begin?
When the soul is forged in the expanding universe?
When our mother dreams us into the ocean of her body?
Or that quickening leap, zing, and tumble
against the chambers of her heart?

Storm surge. Flood tide.
We fall into our father's arms
and take our place
in the ancestral line
of ordinary time.
First words. First steps.
We answer to our given name,
and learn how to belong.

We are like trees rooting to the shore,
like shushing grasses lulled by wind,
unaware of the mute gray spider
moving among us
unfurling her luminous thread.

That each might bear
the weight of her filament
and be bound in its resonance
one to another.
Through endless blind beginnings
and broken cords,
our lives become a hymn
from earth
to the separating stars.

In Sleep, Some Promise Kept

When the carrier wolves come,
nothing can stop us from falling like water onto their backs.
We bury our cheeks in their fur and breathe in the forest.
Fists clutch the silken folds behind their ears.
Knees on either side squeeze their flanks
as our soft human bellies sink into the swaying spine.
No one has to teach us how to ride.
We learned the smooth animal maneuvers
before our birth, before our eyes,
when we still had tails and nothing to hide.

Something about our bodies now
and the uneven ground of lives lived in electric cities
has caused us to forget the ancient promise.
The treaty lost in shame and ashes long ago.
The other party vanished from our midst.
But the loyal wolves of the Carrier Clan
insist that Darkness will not be a shroud.
They sneak into our palaces and prisons,
lift us from our beds of roses or nails
and carry us like cargo on the zigzag path
between the trees, across the wind-stripped plains,
up through the glacial scree of a high mountain pass
to the shores of the endless lake
where we throw stones at our own reflections
and try in vain to wake the Creator
from his mudbound sleep.

Barefoot in the Dust of a Dream

A paddy wagon unlocks its hinged back.
Ropes untie themselves and I slide down
into warm gray ash, my legs already running.
By day, I'm a fugitive on the open road,
a victim of the man in snakeskin boots.
Tonight, I'm an athlete
alone in a race with no competitors.

The air is not good.
Each footfall into soft dust releases a puff of smoke.
Words drift from my pockets.
Who made this course? Did my father run it?
My mother? My boy? They are gone
and I am padding deeper into my own dust.

A dry universe clouds my vision,
coats my hair and tongue with talc
and mica sparks of stars I cannot see.
I am far from the city of holy faith,
the blood mountains, the green turtle sea.

But my body hums in this closed circuit.
My heart gallops.
Like a ribbon on a wheel, the track unrolls
within the muscles of my legs.
There is nowhere but here.
An invisible gaze holds me like a kite,
at my breast,
a long taut string.

Rescue

All night I rode in a cream-colored Buick
with chrome-circled gauges on the glossy wooden dash.
I sat alone in the back seat
as the dream maker drove us into the sea.

Now I meet you at the breakfast table
of daytime abstractions.
Words and money. Husband and wife.
Coffee and steel-cut oats.
Raisins taste like nails that rust my teeth,
maybe yours too.
I don't ask about your body.
You don't look at mine.

In the newspaper, the world comes apart
so neatly in sections.
Yours and mine. Us and them.
You notice road repairs on Route 412
and plan another way to keep from losing time.

I want to ask, why save Time?
Isn't Time the one who stole our boy?
We keep blaming the mountain,
the quality of the snow,
the slope, gravity, velocity —
but really, if not for Time,
he could still be sitting here between us,
pouring milk into a yellow bowl.

If I look up from the front page story
of refugees cast out in a leaden sea,
I will see only you through micro molecules

of salt water flooding my eyes.
You, drowning in your own Aegean Ocean,
your private boat as broken as mine by the gale.
And then what?

You leave for work and I come to the part
about twenty-nine bodies washed up on a beach.
The Red Crescent rushing to retrieve the dead
while they still have faces.

I remember my dream ride in the Buick,
the creaking springs coiled under cool worn leather,
the dashboard with its spinning needles.
Every meter, compass and clock
searches wildly for home.

I want to tell you of the moment
my bare foot kicked back the duvet.
I want to ask you what you dream about
when the spiral eye gathers you in.

Animal Soul Longing

I wish you could see the spider
I feel jazz dancing in my ear,
her long jointed legs
lifting and dipping her two-part body
like a Javanese shadow puppet.

I wish you would come close enough
to reach into the weir of my ribcage
and touch the flailing tail of the golden salmon
caught and raised so far from the river
she's forgotten how to swim.
Leap! she tells me. Now!
It kills her that I don't.

Sometimes I feel fur
between you and me.
Thick velvet pelts flash orange
when we meet nose to nose,
tracking the same faint ley line
in opposite directions.

Other times I see crows
gather in your eyes,
beating their wings,
tormenting the kestrel circling in mine.

Or is it the other way around?
I wish you would tell me
who jumps over your brain
and dozes in your belly.
Is there a pool where a dragonfly drinks?

Dahlias for Toni

In memory of Luise 'Toni' Lenel
September 5, 1912 to October 14, 2012

Early in September
the dahlias start to hide their heavy heads.
Crimson, deep yellow, pink and violet-tipped bursts of enthusiasm,
each more jazzy and ridiculous than the last,
sink facedown into lush green cradles
they spent the summer growing.
Fireworks flash in the dark.
Bright new buds pop open
on buried stems of bruised and rotting flowers.

It takes a killing frost
before a gardener can dig the tubers
and store them in the cellar.
All winter long, in paper bags they slowly shrivel
and curl upon themselves like witches' feet.
Come spring, they start to twitch
and sprout fleshy knobs and hairy protrusions,
some with tiny purple leaves folded like wasp wings.
Each tuber knows itself to be a particular flower,
though the gardener has forgotten
who's who.

I miss my old friend Toni.
I wish I could go to her now,
even to that last room on the first floor
of the King's Daughters Home,
where they shaved her chin in the morning
and fed her crushed strawberries in the afternoon.
I would look into the bright intelligence of her blue eyes
and ask once more, "How are you, Toni?"
just to hear her answer in a soft Heidelberg accent,
"I am old! I am very old!"

Ipiutaq, Greenland

All the psalms learned by heart
sound like knock-offs,
and the words of my own invention
are dollar store wine glasses
teetering on pretentious stems.
I keep drinking new information,
pouring out a thousand convincing story lines,
constructing causes for every effect.
Still I haven't built a scaffold
high enough to hang you.

I never asked for a lover.
Only an iron mother
to smack that face on the kitchen wall
and keep the long and short hands
ticking.

But you keep playing
the timeless roar of a high waterfall
in the channels of my ear.
A spit of land above a fjord,
the fire doused,
all the geologists asleep in their tents
with the black torrent
washing away their snores.

I stood alone on the permafrost
when the strings of your robe untied at my throat.
The night sky tore open.
Fields of stars vanished
in rippling curtains of pale light.
Green and purple flares

fluoresced in grayish clouds of other colors
too fleeting to separate.
Ropes of ether arose in one nowhere,
and faded to nothing in another.

No moon.
I couldn't hear my heart beat.
Couldn't feel my feet.
Who can say
if my mouth opened
when the wine of the universe
poured down?

Turkey Vulture in Search of a Dead Groundhog

Your V-shaped shadow wakes Ben.
Barking, he catapults from the porch,
crisscrosses the winter garden
trampling brittle ghosts
of cosmos, lavender and sage
and bursting seeds of brown-eyed Susan.

You teeter and turn above Ben's rising cries.
Do your garnet eyes see
how his whirling body churns the air
that lifts your bald-head,
ragged fingered wings?
Is this slow hover
only about a rotting corpse,
or like me are you caught
in the wide arc of this dog's joy?
The zestiness of his chase.
The art of his hunt.
The elegance of the kill.

Like a spoon
Ben stirs everything
in our sky brimmed earth bowl.

May each one eat
and be full.

Sleeping All Night on the Dock

for Ben, September 22, 2019

It was barely autumn in our hemisphere
when winter's Great Dog
dug his deepest hole
and scrambled onto the horizon.
He snapped up the morsel of moon
and with his bushy tail
swept the last leaves
from Haystack Mountain.
The moment his paw touched the lake
the Milky Way slid down his back.
All the stars tumbled in.
But not our bright dog.
His paws never broke the surface.
Never one for swimming,
he walked on the silvery water.
Without a sound
Ben crossed over
wagging
while I slept.

Relativity

Fifty years ago to pass the test,
I memorized the constellations
according to the buildings
on Mount Holyoke's campus.
At half-past seven in mid-November,
Cassiopeia was three thumbs left of Abbey Hall
and Orion's Great Dog hung beside the chapel tower.

But stars can lose their gods,
let go their myths
and strand us in the spaces in between.

What I know of night
I learn while sleeping on my back
in a clearing beside the stone labyrinth
built with my own hands
in the middle of a forest
of ailing ash trees and broken off too-tall poplars,
while all around me
beneath the dark dome sky,
animals I cannot see to name
shine their eyes
and snuffle, grunt, and cry.

The Salt Water Kiss

Poems by Nancy Lee Melmon

A Glass of Water

I would love to live as a glass of water.
Walls protect me.
There is space to move,
and dance.
I have a roof open to the stars.
I can be barefoot.
It is so easy to dream I am a quiet, calm ocean
just resting,
maybe sleeping.
Of course, the love of my life will pick me up
and drink.

Snow Angel

Tonight I'm a Snow Angel.
I've fallen, my arms pinwheels.
It's the month of long, long walks in winter coats.
Nights of bright blue shooting stars.
Our laughter rises in the soft light and the cold air.
You and I, not human anymore.
Now we're two spiraling circles of pure light.
Then you kiss me,
pull me out of the snow.
We lean into the shimmering.
Inhale. Exhale.
The moon has a halo around it,
and so do we.
To the sycamore with bare branches
I might look like a tiny white chapel,
warm, with tall glass windows.
A place an Angel could go to and talk to God
in a quiet voice.

Bullets Faster than Angels

It was a baby naming in a synagogue.
He did not need to ring the bell. Or knock.
The door was open.

As bullets flew faster than angels,
was Robert Bowers hearing the third movement of
Handel's Messiah,
where Paul is teaching
of God's glory?

Maybe as Robert was killing,
as he was wandering in and out of the security of his own mind,
living with the company
of a simple man
looking for the promised land,
he was listening to the passion soaring through the rafters
of the first air, "Comfort Ye, My People."

Maybe his head was filled with thousands of angelic voices
announcing the birth of a boy.
Did Mr. Bowers believe he was being guided?
By angels?

Robert might have thought he was a modern-day shepherd.
A loyal member of the militia.

He had three handguns,
an assault rifle,
and the power of the second amendment.
Surely, he had enough rage to keep his flock safe from a tiny infant,
a ninety-seven year old woman,
two brothers,

and those ugly intruders, the migrants,
who are cunning as wolves.

Did he pray?
He was in a synagogue.
If he was praying, what was his prayer?
A good name for the baby?
An audience with Zeus?
Maybe Handel.

Could Mr. Bowers have forgotten Handel's words,
"God alone should have the glory."

Was he muttering under his breath,
"I absolutely have a right to keep and bear these arms."

Prayers are not enough to pry guns out of clenched fingers.
Guns and rifles do not have minds.
Or hearts.

His neighbors said he was a quiet man,
that he would tell them if they had left their garage door open.

Life, liberty, and the pursuit of happiness
should be more than black-and-white scribbles
in a yellowing manuscript.

Imagine this…
Seven angels of God, shoulder to shoulder across the sky.
Each with their own gun.
They shoot the heart out of the Sun.
The world becomes a cloud.
Do you think we might see that on tomorrow's news?

It would be dark.
How would we see each other's faces?

I Fly with the White Owls

I sleep in a house without a roof,
nothing above my head but the night
and my own set of wings.

My cure for anything
is the courage to leave the branch,
glide silently on the wind,
and fly straight into the darkest places.

Late at night,
I hunt with my second set of eyes.
I find the people who got lost for whatever reason.
A night eagle, I swoop,
into and out the other side.

I sleep in a house where the moon
always holds us,
feeds us soup,
sets any crooked or broken bones.

She Can't Stop Smiling

Coated in copper,
her arms are sore, her copper feet, cold, and they are tired.
The Statue of Liberty,
knowing her unalienable rights as a woman,
as a citizen,
to pursue her own life, and happiness,
on January 21, 2018, stepped down from her pedestal,
leaving broken chains,
a sword, and splintered chairs
off Ellis Island,
to walk over dark waters
and volunteer at the nearest soup kitchen.

Her arms are sore.
Her feet, clad only in sandals, are cold and misty blue.
She can't stop smiling,
as she stands to the left of Governor Cuomo
for nine hours, doling out
coffee, tomato soup and rye bread
into paper bowls and cups —
Cuomo in his gray sweats,
and Lady Liberty with her crown slipping off her brow.

Her arms are very happy,
not from having held her gold leaf torch,
or her tablet,
but from being so close to so many hungry people
smiling at her,
hugging soup bowls to their chest,
sipping hope.

That Long Flat Bone in the Middle of Our Chests

The sternum,
that long flat bone
in the middle of our chests,
can look like a tie
or a prehistoric clumsy fork.
I think our sternums are the polished rose quartz set of spoons
we'd discover in the kitchen drawer of a healer.
The one who sees the heart
as a didgeridoo.

The End of Summer

I think she's in her bare feet.
There is so much light on her face.

Summer yawns.
She whips off her sunglasses, waves,
throws her hands up to the sky,
maybe in prayer,
and the white, pink and blue asters she was clutching
fly like seagulls.

She presses her toes into the wet, damp earth,
and whirls on her heels.
Slips into a new dress of dark red
and lavender,
with handfuls of French violets all around the hem.

She follows the muddy path down the cliff,
an old lantern swaying
at her hip.

The Half Truth

It takes two trains and one bus to get home.
I step off the first train
at Union Station
and hear a half truth snoring.
I smell dried urine,
maybe a cat's,
and I follow the stench of rotten eggs.

The half truth is in a corner,
huddled up against an empty take-out carton
of beef lo mein
and two tired pages
torn from a yellowed December newspaper.
Its head is bald,
a wart over its left eye,
and a few drops of black blood trickle from its ears.
It is sleeping under the moldy seven-year-old story
of Sandy Hook
and the conspiracy theory,
its nose pressed to an air vent,
its back legs twitching, jerking, and shaking.

I've just stepped off the first train
from my nine-to-five job.
I file books at Georgetown Public Library,
and my hands feel too heavy
from remembering
the twenty children's hearts that stopped beating
because it was snowing too heavily
in one person's mind.

Tonight, I want to know
if the Ice Queen still reigns.
I wave my hands in the air,
lit like flares or firecrackers.
I grab the half truth by its skinny shoulders
and shake it.
 "Wake up!"

The Old Apple Tree

Mom is dying.
She's a withered old apple tree,
bent over from drinking the North Wind for ninety-two years
out of paper cups.
A victim of too many Vermont frosts
stockpiled in her lungs,
like muskets
saved from the Civil war.

Mom is a hoarder.
The queen of the hard, stony, cold black stare,
and the firm belief
that bitter dandelions
and big pots of scalding, boiling water
with slices of lemon
will cure loss.

Her eyes can bore into your core
like an aphid.
Love was a morning ritual tablespoon of cod liver oil.
Gratitude was a nickel and a dime
in the palm on Monday morning.
Sorrow was not allowed to bloom in her garden,
only in her children.

The old white rose bush
leaning against her kitchen window
spoke fluent French,
a language their collie dug up one day,
from an early memory
she buried.

That white rose knew my Mother.
To survive, she needed
days of full sun and hummingbirds
building nests in the neighborhood.
Grecian vases of hydrangeas
on the night stand by her bed
to comfort her when she cried
and kissed the pillow my father used to fluff
and shape.

This past last week,
Mom has been shivering and shaking.
The North wind has claimed her as his own.
I rub Manuka honey from local beekeepers —
the same bees who came to the house
and stung her —
into the black crevices running
down her legs.

We lift her
after she dies, and her feet slide so easily,
so willingly
into her body bag.
They are like two thin sticks of melted butter
left out on the porch railing,
soft from the hot sun,
so tired of reading the local news,
tired of trying
to change the minds of the younger generation.

The rest of her body
flows like creek water into a jar.
She would have smiled
if her white lips
weren't so cracked, so dry, so brittle.

The smell of light pink apple blossoms,
spicy and a little smoky,
like an early spring,
much earlier than usual in Vermont,
twists my hands into wet dishrags.
Out the window, freshly discovered patches
of violets and lilies of the valley.
I mop my brow
and stare out at the rain
pounding the roof of the red gazebo.

This Light Green Bug Walking
on My Yellow Writing Pad

It's as tiny as an eyelash.
I see no fear. No trembling of back legs.

I imagine its little brain not worrying about the bigness
of humans, and hands,
and how quick we can strike sometimes.

It's walking with such presence,
like a peacock,
or a young Egyptian woman slowly walking to the Nile,
wading into the water
to fill her jar.

Oh no, excuse me,
and here I've been thinking I was the spiritual one.

Wildflowers, Bach, and a Deer in Sun Valley

Five days and six nights
in the bright, clear thinking, lucid Idaho mountains,
in a valley of Sun.

A deer walks past the window
and then the open sliding glass door, down to the creek
the thick grass wet,
the Sun on it only a few minutes old,
still very sleepy.

I know this deer is wild,
not mine.

Still, it stops to breathe near me
and gazes
at the moist, tranquil space between us,
ears twitching,
as if we are very close friends,
or sisters.

Suddenly, I appreciate
not just the deer, but all who walk on two legs
and four legs,
all the red-tailed hawks,
and peregrine falcons who fly through the sky.

This planet is a magic carpet,
flying through an endless night of stars.

I remember I too am a shaman.
And the world
aches.

My chest is full of words,
millions of lonely people wrapped in wool sweaters,
and a tall glass of cool, dark
spring water.

On the radio,
Bach emerges as a cloud of dust,
then a hurricane.
I can hear his voice in my ear,
in the way he arranges his notes, and trills in this fugue,
reminding me our planet is still innocent
like the deer,
calm and devoted
to every bit of dirt and rock and earth
and hope.

Ladybug on a Sunflower

Twenty people are coming for lunch.

At Safeway,
on my way to pick up an avocado,
I stop at the sunflowers.
A red and green hummingbird
nobody else can see darts out of aisle four,
past my cart, which is occupied
with rye bread, cucumbers,
and me, trying to find two or more cases of happiness
on sale as an appetizer
to accompany the homemade lemonade.

The hummingbird hovers
before a sunflower.

At this moment,
I'm not sure I want to be me.
I would rather be a ladybug,
at the center of a sunflower
in the bunch I will pick for the table.

The Responsibilities of an Electric Toothbrush on Your Daughter's Wedding Day

There you are in the bathroom,
sheets of sweat dripping from your armpits.
The day is still so young,
like a newborn
or a calico kitten curled up in the front porch rocker
to dodge the heat.

Heat that knows your secrets.
Passion and the smell of fresh cut peaches
and plums
linger on your skin.
The word *trust* is tattooed in red
under your left breast.
Not everyone's last name will be changing at the end of this day.

This is the month for lovers
and rosy skin.
Young women in white, vowing "til death us do part."
Boys combing their hair in the mirror.
Lace, tulips, and masses of people
who will tell you to smile
and not cry
every time you think
of letting go of those tiny fingers.

The morning light in the bathroom
gazes at you with soft eyes
as if you were a dandelion,
or a ten-year-old playing the violin
by the creek on a Saturday afternoon.

You know how it feels
to want to walk away from this day.
You hunger just to stand under the shower
with your head thrown back,
and feel the water pouring over your neck muscles,
your shoulders,
and down
to the small of your back.
But now it's time to put the lilac dress
next to your husband's suit.

In its holder,
the toothbrush salutes you.
A toy soldier
with a cool smile and a raised eyebrow.

Spit into the sink
any long-standing pockets of indecisiveness or fear.
Brush your pearly whites
till they shine.

The morning is ready to lift up the corners of your mouth
with its baby fingers.
Be as light as a field of tall proud milkweeds in June.
Make a wish.

Maybe your father will sit down next to you
in one of those white folding chairs.

You Are the Umbrella with the Jersey Cows Grazing on It

(after reading "Litany" by Billy Collins)

You are not fond of mud,
except when it rains.

You are my umbrella.
Not my morning news and coffee
or the black mailbox.

The day is daring you
to leap out of our front door closet
and start chasing the clouds as if they were foxes.

But my dear friend, you and I,
are content to walk and talk with meadows, oaks trees,
and country lanes.

You are my happy dance,
that huge patch of blue sky only an umbrella can see.

You've never been my gold L.L. Bean rain jacket.
Or the size ten purple ankle-length Forecaster.

You have never been
a sissy, rusty front door cow foot scraper.

You are a shady landscape
of red barns,
white picket fences, sweet strawberry patches,
and wide-eyed daisies
a cluster of Jersey cows are munching.

You are sleepy stone walls.
And hundreds of sunflowers.
You could be the Sun. I wonder.

"Slow down," my cow umbrella says.
Taste the raindrops.

I love when my umbrella opens,
that soft milk smell of Jersey cows contentedly grazing.

And me?
I am the winding dirt roads that lead to the red barns
and the tan silos
behind the red barns.
I am the dark, dark earth under all rain puddles.
The quiet of stacked hay.

I have never been two red maples by the swimming hole.

I am a stone fence
and fields of clover where deer graze.
I am the apple grove
where the Jersey cows huddle when it storms.

I am the wild carrots,
the turnips, sage, parsley and cucumbers.
And I am the earthworms that break down the grasses.

I am the yellow towel that dries the dog
after his long swim
in the lake,
the large white dog bed
in the living room,
the leather leash hanging by the front door,
and the round blue collar
with the yellow hearts.

Fact: I am absolutely sure of this one:
"you and me."
A girl and her umbrella.

The Comma

I have a lot of commas. Inside me.
They're quite short.
Thin.
Like twigs.
Yet they have a little round squiggle
at one end.
I build and weave nests out of these little commas
for the birds
that bring me my thoughts.
My thoughts are
my food,
and always, my water.
I write
for the birds that sit in these tiny nests,
singing
with the Sun,
the Moon, the Stars
and the warm breezes on their feathers,
and eggs.
If clouds suddenly
bring the
cold
during the day or night,
there's another clear voice singing in the trees.

The Salt Water Kiss

I think you're part bottlenose dolphin.
Our lips are wet and wild when we kiss,
and your mouth tastes like salt water.

I start believing
I can breathe normally
no matter what may happen,
my body spacious, unfurled like a sail in summer
as I lean into you,
and trust the night breeze, the swirling,
the whirling, your lips, and the tide.

Every time I close my eyes to kiss you,
I see mermaids and slivers of light
from the bright blue glow
of opalescent waves and the Moon,
these women of the sea
who appear between the hours of dusk and dawn,
sitting together on the rocks
by the coral reefs off the lagoon.

Swimming in clear water
under our bare feet
are thousands of pairs of tiny butterfly fish,
spotted and striped
black, orange, yellow,
red and silver.

The sea is a strange place just before dark;
it vibrates.
I feel open and overcome
with the moist language of ocean mist

and green sea foam.
My belly is quivering with desire,
our kiss flowers.
We know how to make light glitter,
and shimmer.

The electric blue starfish,
fallen stars,
are watching us with their one eye
at the end of their five arms.
Ocean stars, five wishes
we whispered to each other.

As if we had wings
to break the sound barrier and fly with the angels
for a few precious minutes
every time we have to breathe
and surface for air.

The power of our kisses
knocks me off my feet like a rogue wave.
I laugh, arch my tail,
flex my back, point my nose down,
and dive.

Ancient Rains

Poems by Angie Minkin

Ancient Rains

The taxi bumps hard
over ruts, rocks, and gravel.
I know the turn-off, says Edgar, our taxi driver.
We decide to believe him,
as we search for the *cenote* —
Mayan source of water and life.

One last turn reveals a spark of blue.
We pay a few pesos to the old man
guarding the entrance to the steep cavern.
Or is it a chasm?
Unsettled, we spiral down broken stairs,
grope for missing rails,
grab trailing vines.
It's ok, you whisper.

We plunge off
that last missing step
into the rains of a thousand summers.
Tiny fish flash like cyan stars
and silk over my breasts, belly, hips.
We kiss, clinging to dark mangrove roots
tangled at the cavern's indigo edge.
Drift back to center in turquoise-clear water,
lift our eyes to the empty sky.
We bind our bodies in a sunlit Mayan cross.

Fortress of Flowers

The mothers of the world link arms and march.
We wrap ourselves in shawls of purple and turquoise
and carry candles, roses, and babies.
We melt church gold and steel bullets.
We build a fortress to shelter bruised children.

We draw warm baths and prepare delicious soups
stuffed with tomatoes, corn, beans, a bit of chile.
We fill our fortress with lullabies,
and the children begin to sing.
We paint walls magenta and bright orange,
as ravens etch stars on the ceilings.

Bougainvilleas and marigolds
burst from our hearts.
Our tears weave silver vines
to protect this garden of souls.

La Reina

I am the queen of my family.
My name is *La Reina*.

I sit on my throne of cardboard boxes,
offering candy and pastries for sale.
You call me *señora*.

I sit like a lizard, nearly asleep
until you come forward.
I rhumba over to bargain with you.

What will you pay for red lollipops,
Valentine cupcakes for *Dia del Amor*?

My head is bowed with age,
gray hair sparse and braided.
My breasts hang heavy and loose.

You see only a snaggle-toothed
old woman with dirty bare feet.

My eldest daughter carefully wove
the purple shawl that keeps me warm.
My grandsons watch over me
as they play music in the square.

I gladly give the money I earn
to my youngest grandchild
for shoes, books, school uniforms.
She will have a different life.

Havana Never Sleeps

Addled by the blood moon,
a rooster crows at 3 a.m.
A street peddler sings his wares —
biscuits and *cafecitos*
for workers returning home
in the wee hours.
We toss and turn on a narrow bed
swaddled with sweaty sheets,
hang over our tiny balcony
that threatens to crumble.
Havana never sleeps.

Sustained by two *mojitos* a day,
we trace Hemingway's path.
We follow the *Malecon*, the beach wall,
to *El Morro*, the fortress guarding the bay.
Lovers whisper, entwined on top of the stone wall.
Old men heave fishing nets into the blue Caribbean.
Blasting radios lead us to domino players
who balance the board on their knees.
They hoist bottles of rum — a party on every corner.
Long-legged women in stilettos and tight red capris
rhumba with beautiful men in perfect white trousers.

Music spirals around us.
Toddlers master salsa rhythms,
as they sway on their papas' shoulders.
Conga players lead the laughing throng
through crowded streets.
We can't resist the wailing trumpets and trombones
and join the elders who cha-cha
on Havana's narrow cobblestones.

Hands and hips pulse with snare drums
and the sharp, syncopated Afro-Cuban beat.
Our tight American bodies melt
and we mambo into Cuban dreams.

The Shallow End

My mother tugs a one-piece swimsuit
over my square little body.
Lockers clang, ladies' loud talk —
sharp odors of sweat and chlorine
sting my nose.
My heart pounds through my chest.
I have to pee.

Just breathe, says my mother, *breathe.*
She sits on a bench with the other parents,
wrapped in a new white robe,
arms folded, mouth stick-straight.

Patti wears a dark blue Speedo,
chews gum and giggles.
Bouncy with a blond flip,
she teaches us to blow bubbles,
kick hard, float in her arms.
My heart slows – my smile is wide.
My arms and legs are blue under water,
and I never want to stop swimming.
My mother wraps me in a big towel,
perches me on the bench, legs swinging.

Your turn, Esther.
Esther?
My mother is getting in the pool?

She peels off her robe,
walks slowly to the shallow end.
Patti's voice is gentle: *let's start with a sip of air.*
I hold my breath as my mother sinks,

grips the pool edge,
tries to lower her face in the water.
Tears roll down her cheeks.
She tries again.
Just breathe.

How to Prepare Stuffing

Every year I pull out your stuffing recipe.
The scratch paper is yellowed, hand-scrawled,
but your instructions are clear and precise.

Sauté fresh breadcrumbs in butter.
Make corn bread from the Jiffy mix.
(Don't eat too much!)
Finely dice onion and celery.
Carefully measure the sage and poultry seasoning.
Add two eggs and broth to moisten.

Your writing looks like mine.

You went off to work early that chilly morning.
Too lazy to say goodbye,
I heard you leave.
You left minestrone soup for my lunch
in my favorite little white enamel bowl.

I'd like to ride a beam of light
to that long-ago morning.
I'd shake that selfish girl
out of her warm bed
to give her mother a kiss goodbye.

I panicked this morning
when I couldn't find your notes.
My heart cracked like the little white bowl,
cast aside when the house was sold.

When I could breathe again,
I remembered to look in the drawer
where I keep hidden treasures.

To begin the ritual, I pull out the old yellow mixing bowl.
Our molecules merge like tiny crystals.
I look in the mirror and see your face.

Night Watch

You spread your mother's yellow tablecloth
over white stratus clouds lined with silver.
A mirror of your wedding china in my cabinet.

You summon me and I float up.
You pour white chrysanthemum tea
in beautiful thin cups.
Tiny flowers open as you extol
their healing properties and inhale deeply.

Fragrant steam surrounds us.
Still, I see the lines on your face.
You are wearing your favorite lavender dress,
deep V-neck, double-breasted white buttons,
elbow-length purple silk gloves.

Why so surprised? you ask
as we touch foreheads.
I've been here all along,
keeping an eye on you and your family.
We're the same age now.

You were always so timid in life.
Now you tap dance across streams.
Leap, you whisper in my ear.
I'll be watching.
I'll ride with you the rest of the way.

Water Birth

We dive into the sea, little swimmer,
casting our fate on the North Pacific gyre.
Oceans echo the tides in our hearts.
Your pulse vibrates with my pulse,
vibrates with your grandmother's pulse.
We call the *amas*, strong Japanese women,
diving for pearls among mermaids,
their headscarves embroidered with lucky symbols.
We call on their strength.

The *amas* dive deep to loosen my legs.
Their breath, long-held, expands my heart.
Their sharp whistles summon dolphins,
the midwives of the sea.
The dolphins circle to catch you
and stretch your cord.
They lift you to the surface
for your first breath.
Their clicks and whistles soothe your cries,
as they dance in joyous flips
to announce your birth.

This is what I wish.
Instead, you are carved from me
in haste under bright lights.
Pounding heart. Streaming eyes. Knotted cord.
I reach through incubator portals to touch you,
and your tiny fins grasp my gloved fingers.
You gaze at me with dark dolphin eyes,
seashell mouth whistling softly
as you breathe through iridescent tubes.

Still, our pulses sing together to the *amas*.

Finding the Way

for Jake

At three, you knew the way
to the blue water tower
high in the hills behind our house.
You sang to the ravens and gulls,
threw stale bread to the ducks,
chattered all the way home.

At twenty-two, you knew the way
to the blue islands in Hawaii,
explored exotic plants,
swam with green turtles.
You saw new land forming
as Pele threw tears around.

At twenty-five, you found your way
to the high desert,
vaulted over rattlesnakes,
camped on harsh islands
to count wild boars and bald eagles,
sent home pictures of Dr. Seuss plants.

Now you've found your way
to an urban bungalow, a steady life.
You plant green saplings,
form careful berms of protection.
You dig deep in hidden soil
to spread roots in a city of concrete.
Your blue eyes seek beauty in cracked places.

The Healing Temple

for Aly

Your daughter rests her heart in your hand.
She is shaky and stunned, like a wren striking a window.
You know what you must do for your fire girl.

Lead her to the stone temple in your secret grove.
Drape the Goddess altar in red and purple silks.
Implore Kali and Oya to show her the way.

Chant to the waning moon.
Breathe with her until she falls asleep.
Weave owls into her dreams.

At dawn, gird your girl
with amethyst and lapis lazuli.
Join hands in the lotus mudra.

Embrace her as she takes wing,
strong as a red-tailed hawk,
wild to claim her life as a woman warrior.

Old Lovers in an Older House

We've been lovers for forty years.
We still dance slow.
Life moves so fast.
We strolled with gleeful babies,
who giggled when we raced.
We ran with kids on bikes,
as they chanted the mantra you taught them:
I know how to ride a bike, I know how to ride a bike.
We white-knuckled the San Francisco hills
with new drivers and bought many new clutches.

So much life lived in the walls
of this little saltbox house.
100 years old and showing its age —
earthquake cracks,
shreds of ancient paisley wallpaper.
We burned white sage
in my mother's abalone shell;
smudged the corners and shadows
to purify the space and dispel drugged ghosts.
We splashed sun on the walls upstairs
and warm green in the kitchen
to bring the trees inside.
Our kids have never known another home.

We're aging fast now —
those steep steps stare us down.
Is that the shadow of a pale horse?
You beat the drums.
I'll burn more sage.

Elegy for a Younger Self

Even after forty-two years,
I'd know that house —
sagging couches on a sagging porch,
side room hidden
by overgrown bushes.

Those bushes are gone now,
but the body remembers.
Orange tiger lilies and purple freesias
bloom in humid summer sun.
White clematis trails across church walls.
Secret acts of violence, buried,
become fertility of a kind.

A breeze riffs through maple branches
hanging over freshly turned soil
in the old cemetery.
Young ghosts walk the streets in cut-offs,
tiptoe silently in the empty town.
The air carries salt of old sweat,
lost dreams.

Alchemy

Maceo's sax wails
as we groove south on I-5.
It's all about love.

We merge with semis and SUVs
to navigate that clogged artery.
Burnt leather buffalo ridges dwarf us.
We seek misty mountains through haze.

We meet at rest stops and gas stations.
Can we hold the joy?

Asian toddlers with bowl haircuts
clutch boxes of blueberries,
chase each other around their mother —
can't stop giggling.

A gap-toothed Indian grandmother,
regal in her green-gold sari,
links arms with her granddaughter.
The blue-jeaned teen never looks up.
Her thumbs flash as she texts on her iPhone.

We share a table with a beautiful Iranian family —
diaphanous scarves and haunting brown eyes.
Their elaborate picnic of dolmas and babaganoush
shames our plebian turkey sandwiches.

I play peek-a-boo
with a giggly Latina *niña.*
Her mama beams
and smooths the baby's red ruffles.

Her hands are golden brown;
mine a mottled pink.
Just an accident of birth.
Our hearts move to the same rhythms;
our roots merge in deepest earth.

Dayenu

Blessed is the flame that burns in the heart's secret places
— Hannah Senesh, *A Social Justice Haggadah*

Our bones sing
with ice-blue mountain streams
flowing past purple columbines
so fragile they break our hearts.

We fill the house with early lilacs
as we honor ancient spring rituals.
We grind bitter herbs,
pretend our tears well from their sharp bite.
We sing the old songs and open the door
for strangers and missing spirits.

We gather around you, dear nephew,
and clasp hands in the dusk.
We whisper hope in your ears,
sing strength into your bones.
We cast spells to banish star-shaped cells,
chant prayers — white blooms of hope.

We dream of salvation
but settle for tiny miracles.
Next year, will we be together
huddled beneath blooming branches?
If we are all together, still singing,
it will be enough.

Release

for Jeanene

It's time now.

We come together,
as sisters always do.
You're in the shadows
trying to find the light.

We bathe you with lavender water,
weave freesias in your sparse hair.
We soothe you with white sage lotion,
dress you in softest cotton.
You are translucent.

Sparrows sing outside your window.
We murmur Irish lullabies,
forgive everything.
We circle your bed with cowry shells,
marigolds and white tapers.

We gather around you,
whisper Godspeed.
You hum farewell to each of us,
ready now for your journey.

As you leave, the candles flicker.

Stars in the Tree Teepee

Slide behind the rain curtain.
Follow the winding trail
to the birch branch teepee,
dripping with moss.
Find light with every footstep.
Seek blessings from the west wind.

Crawl inside your new home.
Swirl seven times in each direction.
Release your gnarled roots
and lace your loom with lichen tendrils.
Braid stars into your prayer shawl.
Weave green memories for your daughters.

Chant the song of your next life.

Snapshots from the Album of the Half-Empty, Half-Full Glass

Poems by Suzanne Dudley

Aside from the Yogi, the Rabbi, the Priest, the Shaman

If a mantra is a sacred utterance,
could it be the Divine scatters it
like sparks from a great fire —
ephemeral and yet eternal?

Who would deny the sacredness
of a birdsong?
The quickening heart of first life? First love?
The scuttle of a crab across sand?
Autumn aspen leaves, a dazzle of sequins
draped on the neckline of the mountain?
The scent of frangipani and earth?
The swirling wake of a wooden paddle
pressed through dark, glassy lake water?
The pivot between exhale and inhale?

If we cannot grasp
the mantras like mangoes hanging ripe,
what are we listening to?

Always Toward Light

*"In order to see birds, it is necessary to become
a part of the silence."*
— Robert Lynd

To see the trees,
drink mineral water through your feet,
eat sunshine to make color,
gather raindrops in your robes,
and imperceptibly stretch
in four dimensions every day.
Root and go deep.
Bend without snapping,
and always grow toward light.

To see the dog,
love with an ivory heart.
Smell hate and fear
and be wary of it.
Let joy wriggle in your body.
Run flat out when you can.
Protect your family
with a wide stance and low growl.
Wag your tail.
Tell tales with your eyes.

To see the child,
use small fingers
to poke, dig, and sample.
See the way alpenglow
awakens the earth.
Pull up, stand, and fall
again and again and again
the way the sun and moon
play chase around the earth.

In order to know,
listen as if you are the frosted grass
reaching for the falling yellow leaf.

Snapshots from the Album of the Half-Empty, Half-Full Glass

1.
He talks to himself outside the CVS pharmacy,
ambles and rambles about police reports
and rabbits, gibbered clips of sound.
He gulps 2-liter bottles of soda,
burps, mumbles, and walks
half in, half out.

2.
The whirring pump
of Fox News
laces the water in her house.
Panic pumps in her veins;
electric jolts jab her mind.
She is convinced,
as worry warps her forehead.
She runs the tap again,
fills a cup to share
an offer of black-and-white love.
She climbs the glass walls.

3.
Each day, I am an ant
amid cyclones and riots
in search of
the athlete's zone
the jazz musician's pocket
the sweet spot
where the noise falls away.
I want to walk the rim
like a wet finger on a goblet
and hear the crystal sing.

It's Never What You Think

1.
He didn't say he was worried about her
when she didn't feel right,
when her belly bloated for no reason,
when her appetite withdrew like a tide.

Panic poisoned the sunrises,
dread drenched the sheets at night,
sadness unbuckled his routines,
and he was scared
when she no longer rattled her toothbrush
in the cup to rinse it like usual.

That's when he knew
she was dying.

2.
It wasn't because the tree house had an enviable view —
with working windows from a salvage lot
and a rope and pulley system
to deliver messages and sandwiches.
It wasn't that it had tight seams
and fine fir boards.
It wasn't even how it invited
the nip of night air
and taste of wildness, of sleeping out
under the starry blanket of dark sky.

Their father spent three years,
a few hours each weekend,
building their dream.
Together, he, the brother and sister

drew plans, held the tape measure,
dropped nails into his big paw of a hand.
His soft voice like crepe paper
frames the memories
they will carry to their desks,
their solitary walks along a river,
or in the whispers to a lover
beneath a silky moon.

Gliding up the Path of April

Two black crows strut
across patches of white snow.
A cluster of purple crocus tips
rises from the damp earth.
Birds chitter, call and sing.
All around me, spring bounces,
but my heart lags, pumping gray winter,
starving and yet resistant to the Apollonian hope
in the deep blue sky.

The knife-like memory of late fall
cuts me still —
how the sun looked over its shoulder at me,
drifted away and lured the geese south —
an indifferent friend, leaving me behind.

I turn away from the chilly thoughts,
choose to notice
a glow caress a birch branch
and kiss the new buds like children.
A cloud passes, and then —
the warmth on my cheek,
and I recognize this tenderness.
My shoulders lower, knees loosen,
the grip on my heart gentles.
I glide up the path of April,
sidle up to longer days,
slip off yesterday,
and melt into the arms of this moment.

If We Could Talk

Was it the August blackberry sun
hinting of another long winter
that tipped you? That made you
choose your own end date?

I have asked these questions
every day to the open air,
to the cracks in the sidewalk,
to the buttons on my coat,
to the heads in a crowd
as I search,
wishing for some miracle,
some fold in time to bring you back.

If I could see you one more time,
I'd listen to your answers,
spill my regrets, my apologies, and my sorrow —
the needlepoint obsessive theories stilled
in final QED.
I'd ask, can you stay for tea?
Talk to me? Let me hear you.
Have some brownies?
My attempt at your recipe —
gooey, laden with chocolate chips.

If they have books in heaven,
what are you reading?
Can you feel it every time
one of us thinks of you?
I hope so —
perhaps that is what makes the day so bright.

Daffodil Lesson

Even the daffodils understand.
When their heads get too big,
they bow them.

Eclipse

I grip your edges.

The map of you
stretched like paper —
belly taut,
breastbone ready to crack.

Through your pinholes,
I glimpse the Divine
without burning my eyes.

The Smell

No matter whether she washes, vacuums, or scrubs
she cannot get rid of the smell of death.
It's in her clothes, her hair, the sofa,
the carpet, her skin, her thoughts.

Pulling weeds from the garden
she remembers other deaths —
Not acrid, not big.
A flicker.
A light beam through a prism.
Breath in, breath out. Stillness.

No, it isn't death that smells, she thinks.
It's the approach. The haunting.
The lurking footfalls, the clothing hanging loose,
the food left uneaten,
the wound that won't scab.

As the sun slips into the envelope of evening,
she glimpses the neighbor
holding his baby to his chest,
taking in the new moon.
She hears the river water lapping
at the old yellow rowboat.
And the smell?
It's just a soft spot in the wooden planks
between the water and the air.

Lines

When my skin was smooth
and few habits tracked deep paths,
I used to think wearing make-up
or getting a remodeled nose
was tantamount to false advertising.
I went barefaced and bump-nosed
in determined self-acceptance
to avoid an awkward reckoning
of my genetics revealed
in a morning-clean face
or the features of my children.

Now, the sum of my laughter,
grief, dismay, surprise,
each yes and no
resides in my wrinkles.
Vanity, like the Kraken monster,
rises, roils, whips its tail,
jaws agape at my aging visage.

Is sagging part of being sage?
A trial of character to withstand time's prank?
As we grow comfortable in our skin,
is it because it's merely looser?

Daily, I ask
how many hours and dollars must I dedicate
to chasing the mirage of my previous reflection?
Purveyors of beauty products tap a vein
dark with longing.
They offer magic nips and tucks,
pulls and plumps,

corrections, injections.
All promise erasure,
and miraculous manacle on time and gravity.

Do I continue to shackle my pride
and manage my growing invisibility?
Trust that a master artist,
like the creator of the Nazca lines,
performs slow detail work on every face,
etching magnificence
when viewed from the right perspective?

Yes, I'd like to believe, this October day
a painter daubed red, orange, and yellow
on trees and lawns,
and with another brush on my face
inked a line of awe.

The Light Within

Certain things she loves for no reason.
The clink-clink of the buckle
on her left boot when she walks.
The sloped back of the stone rabbit
in her neighbor's yard.
The rain sluicing down the gutter.
The smell of the cold in the dog's fur.

Random archives.

Filaments
conducting love,
we light the universe.

Spring Composition from a Slow Dog Walk

I collect the symphony.
Spool house finch melody
with robin and chicadee harmonies.
Forget-me-nots adagio,
then an arc of bleeding hearts spilling
into a cadenza of lilacs and apple blossoms.

The recycling truck rumbles timpani —
clangs, bangs
amid a tremolo of coral tulips.

Rondos hum in the azalea bushes
as pollen-drunk bees
bumble in and out of blooms.

Later between cool night sheets,
I unwind and wind,
layer and replay the music.

Through an open window
chartreuse leaves applaud.

His and Hers

His secrets embedded in his skin,
almost unnoticeable slivers.
They grew
and turned inside out
into lies. Leaked and absorbed
until he believed them.
They replaced truth
and spoke for him.

She kept her secrets
all over.

One in a brown knot
of an old pine plank floor
when she was nine.

She stashed two secrets in a potted plant
at a fraternity party.

Three she scattered
in the morning dew
after a fierce storm.

None of them belonged to her
except the ones in her chest
of drawers
between a lace bra
and her mother's handkerchief.

The Moon in Therapy

after Ho Xuan Huong's "Questions for the Moon"

Do you like being called Diana?
Do you like the wolf's serenade?

How does it feel to be eclipsed?
When *you* eclipse, do you laugh?

Tell me about your phases.
Do you mind living in constant change?

Are you ashamed of your dark side?
Are you jealous of the sun?

How was it to be landed upon?
Do you yearn for boldness?

I realize you lead,
but when you dance with the ocean,
is it love?

Last night as you nestled in the branches
and whispered into the November wind,
did you notice
the crisp oak leaf doing a jig?

Cello in the Woods

She rests her *mejilla* — her cheek — on the rough bark,
listens to cello chords in the thick trunk.
Harmonies tumble down the curve of time.

Music floats, flutters, shimmies
into a pair of navy slacks
drying on a rope line,
strung like a necklace
between two collarbones of brick buildings.

The pants belong to a gray man
who calls the crows
angelita, mi amor, querida.
He feeds them crusts and Sunday comics.

Twice a day he shuffles in sandals —
soles worn smooth and thin as his skin,
into the walled garden and visits
memories tucked between thick aloe spikes
and the scraggly legs of pale roses.

Today, the wind rattles
the "Mom's Garden" plaque
hanging on the rusted fence.
Segovia suites whisper
through the gray man's sleep,
flavor his dreams with Spanish brandy.

Your Prayer for Wings Is Not Wasted

If only you could know.

How your hunger feeds you.
How your shedding grows you.

How your inching moves you,
each reach and bend
a supplication.

How your chrysalis walls
bind briefly.
How stillness transforms.

How you will flutter orange and black wings
in a blue September sky
and fly faraway to live
amid fragrant eucalyptus groves.

Glossary for Poems by Angie Minkin

Spanish/English Glossary

Ancient Rains
Cenote — A limestone sinkhole created when a cave ceiling has collapsed; considered a sacred source of water by the Mayans.

La Reina
La Reina — The Queen
Dia del Amor — Valentine's Day

Havana Never Sleeps
Cafecito — A small cup of strong, sweet coffee.
Mojito — A rum drink made with lime juice, mint, and sugar.
Malecon — The seawall that runs along the coast in Havana, Cuba.
El Morro — Fortress and castle guarding the entrance to
      Havana Bay.

Alchemy
Niña — Little girl

Japanese/English Glossary

Water Birth
Ama — "Sea woman" refers to Japanese women famous for diving for pearls without air tanks or other equipment.

Hebrew/English Glossary

Dayenu
Dayenu — It would have been enough. Traditionally sung as a praise song during the Jewish rite of Passover.

Glossary for Poems by Lisha Adela Garcia

Spanish/English Glossary

My Mother Wants Me to Explain

No amamos igual, no sentimos igual
We don't love in the same way or feel the same things.

Calaveras

Calaveras literally means skeletons. It also is a literary form of limericks popular during the celebration of *Día de los Muertos*. Skeletons can't be harmed, so during the Day of the Dead festivities, they write "Truths or *calaveras*" about political figures without fear of repercussion.

Huipiles

Native hand loomed and embroidered dresses and shirts worn by the native peoples of Mexico and Central America.

The Day We Split in Two — Entering the USA

Cordillera — Mountain range

This Stone Will Speak

Quetzal — *Quetzals* are brightly colored birds with iridescent green wings, back, chest and head, and a red belly. They are found in forests in Mexico and the southern United States, close to the Mexican border. Its name means "precious" or "sacred" in several Mesoamerican languages and is considered divine. The *quetzal* is associated with the snake god Quetzalcoatl and seen as a symbol for goodness and light.

Texas Courtship in the Rio Grande Valley

Ven hija — Come daughter.

A New Pond

Kokopelli flute — Kokopelli is a fertility deity, usually depicted as a humpbacked flute player. He is worshipped by some Native American cultures in the Southwestern United States. Like most fertility deities, Kokopelli presides over both childbirth and agriculture.

Gitana — A gypsy girl or woman
Saltillo tile — A type of terra-cotta tile that originates in Saltillo, Coahuila, Mexico.

La Llorona — The Weeper
Mythical woman iconic in Mexican culture. In this poem, *La Llorona* is represented in one of Mexico's most famous songs by the same title.

Three Months in the USA
Quetzalteca — Guatemalan fire water or moonshine

Maria Elena at the Salvation Army
Quinceañera — A rite of passage celebration of a young woman
     at age fifteen.
Veijitas — Old ladies
Trenzas — Braids
Batas — Housecoats
Ándale Magdalena, que Dios te bendiga. Go on Magdalena,
     may God bless you
Saludos — Greetings or give my greetings

Blue Sheets
Frijoles — Beans
Sopa de fideo — Noodle soup
La droga — The drug

Glossary for Poems by Suzanne Dudley

Spanish/English Glossary

Cello in the Woods

Angelita — Little angel
Mejilla — Cheek
Mi amor — My love
Querida — Dear/dear one

About the Authors

Lisha Adela García has an MFA from Vermont College of Fine Arts and currently resides in Texas with her beloved four-legged children. Her books, *A Rope of Luna* and *Blood Rivers*, were published by Blue Light Press of San Francisco. Her chapbook, *This Stone Will Speak*, was published by Pudding House Press. In addition, she is widely published in various journals including the Boston Review, Crab Orchard Review, Border Senses, Muse and Mom Egg Review. Lisha has been nominated for a Pushcart and was recently recognized with the San Antonio Tri-Centennial Poetry Prize. She also has a Masters in International Management from Thunderbird for the left side of her brain.

Jennifer Read Hawthorne is the author/editor of eight books, including the #1 *New York Times* best sellers *Chicken Soup for the Woman's Soul* and *Chicken Soup for the Mother's Soul* and a book of poems, *Life as a Prayer*. Together, her books have sold more than 14 million copies. Jennifer lives in Vero Beach, Florida, nourished by palm trees and ocean.

"Ripening" and "Touchstone" were previously published in *Soul-Lit: A Journal of Spiritual Poetry*. "My Mother's House" was previously published in *On the Veranda Literary Journal*. "Wild Child," "Easter Morning on Black Mountain," "The Yogini," "The Wedding," "Surgical Vision," "Beneath the Radar," "Memorial Day," "Out of Bounds," "Authors Ridge," "The Beauty of Him," "In Search of Mary Oliver," and "Taking My Measurements" were previously published in *Life as a Prayer* (High Tea Press).

Anna Kodama paints, walks, and writes poems in Eastern Pennsylvania, a few miles from the Delaware River. She has raised three children, chickens, and vegetables, taught adult literacy, and written organic gardening books. Even so, she remains that ten-year-old schoolgirl who interrupted the 5th grade lunch count to ask, "How do we know this isn't a dream?"

Nancy Lee Melmon — I believe in poetry, books, angels, and the stars. As a child I heard the stars singing. I thought everyone could.

I was born in Boston and grew up with parents who loved the sea. I live with my husband in Sedona, Arizona, a town of dark skies, a town that used to be an ocean. I remember going to the library with my mother and holding my first library card. It felt warm and happy. I felt full of light, like a candle someone just lit. I don't know where my desire to write came from. The stars? Or one of the books I read as a child? Or my parents when they read me stories from fairy books. Maybe an eagle dropped an inspirational tail (tale) feather into my heart when I was six, and I had to write. I just had to. My writing life is like living with an angel. Or the Goddess of the Sea. Sometimes I don't wade out far enough into the water to be embraced by her, to be covered with her kisses of salt water ... sometimes I do. Then I am floating amongst the stars, so close to her, I can see her breathing.

Angie Minkin — Shaped by mountains and cornfields, Angie Minkin is grateful to live near the sea in San Francisco, California. A poetry editor with *Vistas & Byways Literary Review*, her work has appeared in that journal as well as *The Pangolin Review, Oh Mama, Bach in the Afternoon, The Sky Away from Here*, and *New Verse News*. Angie is inspired by the political landscape, the poetry of liberation, and the voice of the wise woman. Three of Angie's favorite poets are Sharon Olds, Ellen Bass, and Elizabeth Alexander. When not writing, Angie practices yoga, takes dance classes, studies Spanish, and works on political issues. She travels to Oaxaca, Mexico whenever possible. Angie is forever grateful to Diane Frank, Blue Light Press, and her Poet Sisters for their encouragement and inspiration. She dedicates her section of this anthology to her husband and children. They are her everything.

The following poems were previously published in various publications, often in very different forms: "Fortress of Flowers" appeared in *The Pangolin Review* and *Bach in the Afternoon*. "Old Lovers in an Older House" appeared in *Bach in the Afternoon*. "Water Birth" appeared in *Oh Mama* and also earned an Honorable Mention in the Poetry Category of the 2019 Soul-Making Keats Literary Competition. "Alchemy" appeared in *Vistas & Byways Literary Review*. "Elegy for a Younger Self" appeared in *The Sky Away From Here*. "The Healing Temple" appeared in *The Sky Away From Here*. "Dayenu" appeared in *The Sky Away From Here*.

Suzanne Dudley (Schon) lives in New Hampshire with her husband and ever-changing tide of their five children, and squad of geriatric dogs. She works as a life and business coach, committed to helping people "rewrite their stories" and live with greater freedom and playfulness. Suzanne's poems have appeared in *Future Cycle*, *Amore Love Poems*, *Sin Fronteras* and more. She is grateful for the support and belief in her writing from Diane Frank and her fellow poets in this book. She dedicates her section of *Dreams and Blessings* to her children, Connor and Hunter Schon. Her love for them fueled the desire to write poems born from love, offering light, beauty, grace, inspiration, and hope — her best legacy.